In

GIVE THIS BACK TO: .... (AND DON'T TAKE MY PEN!)

DOSAGES

PHONE NUMBERS

REMINDERS

ETC.

NOTES TO KEEP ME SANE

NOTES TO KEEP ME SANE

NOTES TO KEEP ME SANE

NOTES TO KEEP ME SANE

NOTES TO KEEP ME SANE

NOTES TO KEEP ME SANE

NOTES TO KEEP ME SANE

NOTES TO KEEP ME SANE

NOTES TO KEEP ME SANE

NOTES TO KEEP ME SANE

ALL TREES HAVE BARK. ALL DOGS BARK.
THEREFORE, ALL DOGS ARE TREES. THE
FALLACY OF BARKING UP THE WRONG TREE.

NOTES TO KEEP ME SANE

NOTES TO KEEP ME SANE

NOTES TO KEEP ME SANE

NOTES TO KEEP ME SANE

NOTES TO KEEP ME SANE

NOTES TO KEEP ME SANE

NOTES TO KEEP ME SANE

NOTES TO KEEP ME SANE

NOTES TO KEEP ME SANE

NOTES TO KEEP ME SANE

NOTES TO KEEP ME SANE

NOTES TO KEEP ME SANE

NOTES TO KEEP ME SANE

NOTES TO KEEP ME SANE

CAT'S MOTTO: NO MATTER WHAT YOU'VE
DONE WRONG, ALWAYS TRY TO MAKE IT
LOOK LIKE THE DOG DID IT.

NOTES TO KEEP ME SANE

NOTES TO KEEP ME SANE

NOTES TO KEEP ME SANE

NOTES TO KEEP ME SANE

NOTES TO KEEP ME SANE

NOTES TO KEEP ME SANE

NOTES TO KEEP ME SANE

NOTES TO KEEP ME SANE

NOTES TO KEEP ME SANE

NOTES TO KEEP ME SANE

NOTES TO KEEP ME SANE

NOTES TO KEEP ME SANE

NOTES TO KEEP ME SANE

NOTES TO KEEP ME SANE

NOTES TO KEEP ME SANE

NOTES TO KEEP ME SANE

NOTES TO KEEP ME SANE

NOTES TO KEEP ME SANE

NOTES TO KEEP ME SANE

NOTES TO KEEP ME SANE

NOTES TO KEEP ME SANE

NOTES TO KEEP ME SANE

NOTES TO KEEP ME SANE

REMEMBER- YOUR TEAM CAN'T DO THIS WITHOUT YOU! YOU ROCK!

NOTES TO KEEP ME SANE

NOTES TO KEEP ME SANE

NOTES TO KEEP ME SANE

NOTES TO KEEP ME SANE

NOTES TO KEEP ME SANE

NOTES TO KEEP ME SANE

NOTES TO KEEP ME SANE

NOTES TO KEEP ME SANE

NOTES TO KEEP ME SANE

NOTES TO KEEP ME SANE

NOTES TO KEEP ME SANE

NOTES TO KEEP ME SANE

NOTES TO KEEP ME SANE

NOTES TO KEEP ME SANE

NOTES TO KEEP ME SANE

NOTES TO KEEP ME SANE

NOTES TO KEEP ME SANE

NOTES TO KEEP ME SANE

NOTES TO KEEP ME SANE

NOTES TO KEEP ME SANE

NOTES TO KEEP ME SANE

NOTES TO KEEP ME SANE

NOTES TO KEEP ME SANE

NOTES TO KEEP ME SANE

NOTES TO KEEP ME SANE

DOGS BELIEVE THEY ARE HUMAN.
CATS BELIEVE THEY ARE GOD.

NOTES TO KEEP ME SANE

NOTES TO KEEP ME SANE

NOTES TO KEEP ME SANE

NOTES TO KEEP ME SANE

NOTES TO KEEP ME SANE

NOTES TO KEEP ME SANE

NOTES TO KEEP ME SANE

NOTES TO KEEP ME SANE

NOTES TO KEEP ME SANE

NOTES TO KEEP ME SANE

NOTES TO KEEP ME SANE

NOTES TO KEEP ME SANE

NOTES TO KEEP ME SANE

NOTES TO KEEP ME SANE

NOTES TO KEEP ME SANE

NOTES TO KEEP ME SANE

NOTES TO KEEP ME SANE

NOTES TO KEEP ME SANE

NOTES TO KEEP ME SANE

NOTES TO KEEP ME SANE

NOTES TO KEEP ME SANE

NOTES TO KEEP ME SANE

NOTES TO KEEP ME SANE

NOTES TO KEEP ME SANE